If **I** am in Christ, **I** am a new creation; old things have passed away: behold, all things have become new.

- 2 Corinthians 5:17

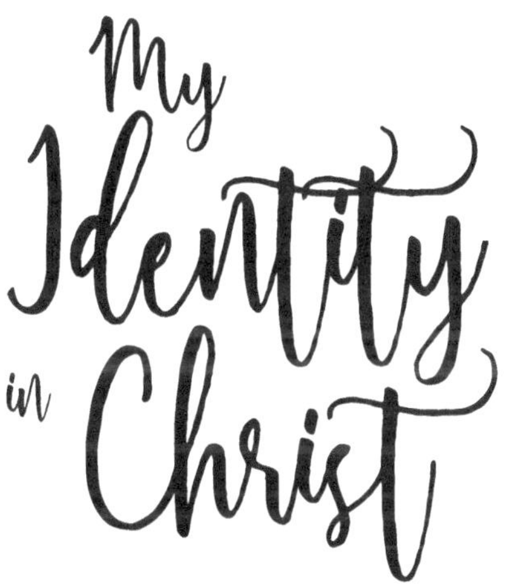

My Identity in Christ

"I am" Declarations
That Reveal Your
In-Christ Realities.

MyVersion Publishing

My Identity in Christ
"I am" Declarations That Reveal
Your In-Christ Realities.

Print Edition
ISBN 13: 979-8-89846-154-6
Copyright © 2026 MyVersion Publishing

Published by: MyVersion Publishing
https://MyVersionBook.com

Contents

Introduction

Your True Identity Revealed

From the very beginning, God's plan for mankind was never confusion, shame, or separation—it was fellowship, sonship, and authority. Through Jesus Christ, that original design has been fully restored. When you were born again, you did not merely receive forgiveness; you became a new creation in Christ. Your identity changed. Your nature changed. Your standing before God changed.

This book is designed to help you discover and declare who you already are in Christ. These scriptures reveal that you are made righteous, accepted, secure, empowered, and victorious, not because of your performance, but because of what Jesus accomplished on your behalf. The Christian life is not about striving to become someone; it is about believing and living from who God says you already are.

These confessions are not positive thinking or self-improvement statements. They are the living Word of God. Faith comes by hearing, and as you continually speak these truths over your life, they will renew your mind and establish your heart in the finished work of Christ. When you see yourself the way God sees you, you will walk differently, pray differently, and expect differently.

No matter what your past has been or what challenges you face today, your identity is now rooted in Christ. You are not defined by failure, fear, or limitation; you are defined by your union with Him. As you read and speak these Scriptures aloud, let them reshape your thinking and strengthen your faith.

Take each verse personally. Declare it boldly. Agree with God. As you do, you will begin to experience the confidence, freedom, and authority that belong to you as a son or daughter of the Most High God.

Part One

I am...
Made New and Alive

I have passed from death to life

Listen closely! If **I** hear the Word of the Lord, and believe on God, **I** have everlasting life, and will not come into condemnation. **I** have passed from death to life.

— *John* 5:24

More Verses

John 3:16; 1 John 5:11-12;
Ephesians 2:1-5

I am alive to God through Jesus Christ

I am fully dead to sin, but am alive to God through Jesus Christ our Lord.

— Romans 6:11

More Verses
Ephesians 2:1-5; Romans 6:4;
Galatians 2:20; Colossians 3:1-3

I am a new creation in Christ Jesus

Therefore, if **I am** in Christ, **I am** a new creature: old things are passed away; behold, all things have become new!

- 2 Corinthians 5:17

More Verses
Galatians 6:15; Colossians 3:9

I am crucified with Christ, and now Christ lives in me

I am crucified with Christ. Yet, **I** live; not **me**, but Christ lives in **me**. And the life **I** live, **I** live by faith in the Son of God who loves **me** and gave Himself for **me**.

- Galatians 2:20

More Verses

Colossians 1:27; Romans 6:6;
Philippians 1:21

I am a new person created in God's image

I put on the new man who was created in God's image. **I am** created in righteousness and true holiness.

- Ephesians 4:24

More Verses

Galatians 5:16; 2 Corinthians 4:16;
Colossians 3:10;

I am a partaker of the divine nature of God

I have been given exceeding great and precious promises: through that, **I** have become a partaker of the divine nature, escaping the corruption that is in the world through greed.

- 2 Peter 1:4

More Verses
2 Corinthians 5:21; John 1:12-13;
Galatians 4:6; 1 John 3:9

I was raised up by the glory of God and I now walk in newness of life

I was buried with Him by baptism into death, now just as Christ was raised from the dead by the Glory of the Father, so will **I** walk in newness of life.

— Romans 6:4

More Verses
John 3:3-6; Titus 3:5; 1 Peter 1:23

Part Two

I am...

Forgiven and Made Right with God

My Identity In Christ

My sins were removed far away

As far as the east is from the west, that's how far God removed **my** transgressions and sins from **me.**

— Psalm 103:12

More Verses
Micah 7:19; Isaiah 43:25;
Hebrews 10:17

My sins were made white as snow

Though **my** sins were as scarlet, they are as white as snow; though they were red like crimson, they are now as wool.

— Isaiah 1:18

More Verses
Psalm 51:7; 1 John 1:7-9;
Revelation 1:5

I am justified by faith and am at peace with God

Therefore, being justified by faith, **I** have peace with God through **my** Lord Jesus Christ.

– Romans 5:1

More Verses
Romans 4:5; Romans 8:1;
Colossians 1:20

I am the righteousness of God in Christ Jesus

For God made Him who knew no sin to be sin for **me**, that **I** might be made the righteousness of God in Christ Jesus.

- 2 Corinthians 5:21

More Verses
Philippians 3:9; Romans 3:22-24;
1 Corinthians 1:30

I am in Christ and have His wisdom, righteousness, sanctification, and redemption

I am in Christ Jesus, who of God is made to **me** wisdom, righteousness, sanctification, and redemption.

— 1 Corinthians 1:30

More Verses

Jeremiah 23:6; Romans 8:30; Hebrews 10:14

I am justified from all things

Because of Christ and because **I** believe, **I am** justified from all things, even from the things that **I** could not be justified of through the law of Moses.

- Acts 13:38-39

More Verses
Romans 3:24-26; Ephesians 1:7;
Colossians 1:14

My sins are remembered no more

For God is merciful to **my** unrighteousness. **My** sins and iniquities He remembers no more.

— Hebrews 8:12

More Verses

Hebrews 10:17; Jeremiah 31:34; Psalm 103:12

I have a clean conscience, cleansed from dead works

How much more will the blood of Christ, who... offered Himself without spot to God, purge **my** conscience from dead works to serve the living God?

- Hebrews 9:14

More Verses
Hebrews 10:22; 1 Peter 3:21;
1 John 1:7

I am sanctified once and forever

I am sanctified through the offering of the body of Jesus Christ once for all.

- Hebrews 10:10

More Verses

Hebrews 10:14; 1 Corinthians 6:11; Ephesians 5:26

I was raised up by the glory of God and now walk in newness of life

I was buried with Him by baptism into death, now just as Christ was raised from the dead by the Glory of the Father, so will I walk in newness of life.

- Romans 6:4

More Verses
John 3:3-6; Titus 3:5; 1 Peter 1:23

I have no condemnation because I am in Christ

There is therefore now no condemnation to **me** because **I** am in Christ Jesus, I walk not after the flesh, but after the Spirit.

— Romans 8:1

More Verses
Romans 8:33-34; John 5:24;
Colossians 2:14

My Identity In Christ

Part Three

I am...

Loved and Accepted as Gods Child

My Identity In Christ

I am loved with everlasting love

The Lord is saying to **me**, "I love you with an everlasting love; with lovingkindness I have drawn you to me."

- Jeremiah 31:3

More Verses

Romans 8:38-39; Zephaniah 3:17; Ephesians 2:4-5

I am loved just as the Father loves Jesus

The world will know that God sent Jesus and loves **me** just as God has loved Him.

- John 17:23

More Verses
1 John 3:1; Romans 5:8;
Ephesians 1:6

I am a child of God by faith in Jesus

For **I am** a child of God by faith in Jesus Christ.

— Galatians 3:26

More Verses
John 1:12; 1 John 3:2;
Ephesians 1:5; Romans 8:15-16

I have the Spirit of Christ in my heart because I am a child of God

And because **I am** a child of God, God has sent the Spirit of His Son into **my** heart.

- Galatians 3:26

More Verses

Romans 8:15-16; 2 Corinthians 1:22; Ephesians 1:13-14

I am free from fear, because I have received the Spirit of adoption

I have not received the spirit of bondage again to fear; but I have received the Spirit of adoption, whereby I cry, Abba, Father.

- Romans 8:15

More Verses

Galatians 4:6; Ephesians 1:5;
Romans 8:16

I am no longer a servant, but a son and heir through Christ

I am no longer a servant, but a son; and if a son, then an heir of God through Christ.

- *Galatians* 4:7

More Verses
Romans 8:17; Ephesians 1:11;
1 Peter 1:3-4

I live through Christ because God loved me first

God showed His love toward **me**, because God sent His only begotten Son into the world, that **I** might live through Him. This is love, not that **I** love God, but that He loves **me**, and sent His Son to be the propitiation for **my** sins.

— 1 John 4:9-10

More Verses

Romans 5:8; John 3:16; 1 John 4:19

I am led by the Spirit of God so I am a son of God

I am led by the Spirit of God, therefore, I am a son of God.

- Romans 8:14

More Verses
Galatians 5:18; John 10:27;
Romans 8:16

Part Four

I am...

Chosen, Called, and Set Apart

My Identity In Christ

My Identity In Christ

I was known and set apart from before I was born

Before **I** was formed in the belly God knew **me**; and before **I** came out of the womb the Lord sanctified **me**, and ordained **me** as a prophet to the nations.

- Jeremiah 1:5

More Verses

Ephesians 1:4-5; 2 Timothy 1:9; Psalm 139:16

I am Christ's friend, all things that He heard from the Father I now know

The Lord does not call **me** a servant; for a servant does not know what their master does. Instead, He calls **me** a friend; for all things that He has heard of the Father, He has made known to **me**.

— John 15:15

More Verses
John 15:13-14; James 2:23;
Hebrews 2:11

I am part of a chosen generation, a royal priesthood

I am part of a chosen generation, a royal priesthood, a holy nation, a peculiar people; so **I** can show forth the praises of the Lord who has called **me** out of darkness into His marvelous light.

- 1 Peter 2:9

More Verses

Exodus 19:5-6; Revelation 1:6; Isaiah 43:21

I am an heir of God and joint-heir with Christ

And if **I am** a child of God, then **I** am an heir; heir of God, and joint-heir with Christ; and if it so be that **I** suffer with Him, **I** will also be glorified together with Him.

— Romans 8:17

More Verses
Ephesians 1:11; 1 Peter 1:3-4; Galatians 4:7

I am called with a holy calling according to Christ's purpose for me

The Lord saved **me**, and called **me** with a holy calling, not according to **my** works, but according to His own purpose and grace, which was given to **me** in Christ Jesus before the world began.

– 2 Timothy 1:9

More Verses

1 Thessalonians 5:24; Hebrews 3:1;
Romans 8:28-30

I am redeemed! God has called me by name, I am His

Fear not: for the Lord has redeemed **me,** He has called **me** by name; **I** am His.

\- Isaiah 43:1

More Verses
Isaiah 43:7; John 10:3; 1 Peter 2:9

Part Five

I am...
Secured in Christ

My Identity In Christ

No one can pluck me out of the Lord's hand

The Lord gives **me** eternal life; and **I** will never perish, neither will any man pluck **me** out of Christ's hand. The Father, which gave **me** to Christ, is greater than all; and no man is able to pluck **me** out of even the Father's hand.

— John 10:28-29

More Verses

1 Peter 1:5; 2 Timothy 1:12

Everything works together for my good, because I love God and am called according to His purpose

All things work together for **my** good because **I** love God, and am called according to His purpose.

- Romans 8:28

More Verses
Ephesians 1:11; Genesis 50:20

I cannot be separated from the love of God

Who shall separate **me** from the love of Christ? shall tribulation, or distress, or persecution, or famine, or nakedness, or peril, or sword?

- Romans 8:35

More Verses

Romans 8:38-39; John 10:28-29; Psalm 23:4

My gifts and callings are irrevocable

For the gifts and callings given to **me** by God are without repentance.

- Romans 11:29

More Verses
Philippians 1:6; Numbers 23:19;
2 Corinthians 1:20

I am established, anointed, and sealed by God with the Holy Spirit in my heart

God established **me** in Christ, and has anointed **me**; He has also sealed **me**, and gave **me** the gift of the Spirit in **my** heart.

- 2 Corinthians 1:21-22

More Verses

Ephesians 1:13-14;
2 Corinthians 5:5; John 14:16-17

I am confident that He who began a good work in me is faithful to perform it

I am confident of this very thing, that He which began a good work in **me** will perform it until the day of Jesus Christ.

- Philippians 1:6

More Verses
1 Thessalonians 5:24;
Hebrews 12:2; Jude 1:24

I am persuaded that God will guard what I have entrusted Him.

…**I** know who **I** have believed in, and am persuaded that the Lord is able to keep that which **I** have entrusted to Him until that day.

- 2 Timothy 1:12

More Verses
John 10:28-29; 1 Peter 1:5;
Psalm 121:7-8

I am saved to the uttermost, because Jesus has interceded for me

The Lord is able also to save **me** to the uttermost since **I** have come to God through Christ, seeing Christ lives to make intercession for **me**.

- Hebrews 7:25

More Verses
Romans 8:34; Hebrews 4:14-16;
1 John 2:1

I am kept from falling. I am seen faultless before God.

Now the Lord is able to keep **me** from falling, and presents **me** faultless before the presence of His glory with exceeding joy.

- Jude 1:24

More Verses
1 Peter 1:5; Psalm 37:23-24;
Philippians 1:6

I am born of God; I am able to keep myself away from sin, and the evil one cannot touch me.

I know that **I am** born of God, and **I** do not continue sinning before Him. He who was begotten of God keeps **me** safe, so that wicked one does not touch **me**.

— 1 John 5:18

More Verses
John 17:15; Psalm 91:10-11; 2 Thessalonians 3:3

I can come to my father for anything and will never be cast out

…When **I** come to Jesus, there is no way **I** can be cast out.

— John 6:37

More Verses
John 6:39; John 10:28-29;
Romans 8:38-39

Part Six

I am...

Victorious in Christ

My Identity In Christ

I have peace and am of good cheer because Christ has overcome the world

In Christ **I** have peace. In the world **I** will have tribulation: but **I** will be of good cheer because Christ has overcome the world.

— John 16:33

More Verses
1 John 5:4; Romans 8:37;
2 Corinthians 2:14

I reign in life through Christ

For if by one man's (Adam's) offense death reigned by one; much more **I**—who have received an abundance of grace and the gift of righteousness—will reign in life by one, Jesus Christ.

- Romans 5:17

More Verses

Romans 8:37; 1 Corinthians 15:57; 2 Corinthians 2:14

I am an overcomer because greater is He who is in me than he that is in the world

I am of God… and have overcome them: because greater is He that is in **me**, than he that is in the world.

— 1 John 4:4

More Verses
1 John 5:4; John 16:33;
Romans 8:37

I overcome the world through faith in the Son of God

Since **I am** born of God, **I** overcome the world: and this is the victory that overcomes the world, even **my** faith. **I** overcome the world because **I** believe that Jesus is the Son of God.

- 1 John 5:4-5

More Verses
John 16:33; Romans 8:37;
Revelation 12:11

I am an overcomer by the blood of the Lamb and the word of my testimony

I overcame the enemy by the blood of the Lamb, and by the word of **my** testimony.

- Revelation 12:11

More Verses

Hebrews 2:14; Colossians 2:15;
Romans 8:37

I am more than a conqueror through Him that loved me

In all these things **I am** more than a conqueror through Him that loved **me**.

- Romans 8:37

More Verses
1 John 4:4; 2 Corinthians 2:14; Revelation 12:11

I have victory through my Lord Jesus Christ

But thanks be to God, which gives **me** the victory through **my** Lord Jesus Christ.

- 1 Corinthians 15:57

More Verses

2 Corinthians 2:14; Romans 8:37;
1 John 5:4

I am free indeed

If the Son makes **me** free, **I** will be free indeed.

- John 8:36

More Verses
Galatians 5:1; Romans 6:18;
2 Corinthians 3:17

I have authority over all the power of the enemy, and nothing will in any way hurt me

Behold, the Lord has given **me** power to tread on serpents and scorpions, and over all the power of the enemy: and nothing will by any means hurt **me**.

- Luke 10:19

More Verses

Mark 16:17-18; Ephesians 6:10-11; James 4:7

Part Seven

I am...
Significant
to the Father

My Identity In Christ

I am fearfully and wonderfully made; I am a marvelous work of God's hands

I am fearfully and wonderfully made… **my** frame was not hid from the Lord… His eyes saw **my** unformed body, when **I** was still being formed; and in His book all of **my** days were written….

- Psalm 139:13-16

More Verses
Ephesians 2:10; Jeremiah 1:5;
Genesis 1:27

I am so valuable to God. Every hair on my head is numbered by Him

Not one sparrow falls to the ground without the Father's care. But the very hairs of **my** head are all numbered. **I** should not fear, **I am** much more valuable than many sparrows.

- Matthew 10:29-31

More Verses
Luke 12:24; Matthew 6:26;
Luke 12:7; Psalm 56:8

My name is written on the palm of the Lord's hand

Look, the Lord has inscribed **my** name on the palms of His hands…

– *Isaiah* 49:16

More Verses

Isaiah 43:4; Deuteronomy 32:10;
Psalm 139:17

I am a member of the body of Christ and was placed there by God

God has set **me** as a member in the body of Christ. He sets **me** and every member as it pleases Him.

— 1 Corinthians 12:18

More Verses

Romans 12:4-5;
1 Corinthians 12:27; Ephesians 4:16

I am raised up together with Christ and sit together with Him in heavenly places in Christ Jesus

God has raised **me** up, and made **me** sit together with Him in heavenly places in Christ Jesus.

— *Ephesians 2:6*

More Verses

Colossians 3:1-2; Romans 8:17;
Ephesians 1:20-21

I have been bought with a price; I belong to God

My body is the temple of the Holy Spirit which is in **me**, which **I** have from God, and is not **my** own. For **I** was bought with a price: therefore **I** will glorify God in **my** body, and in **my** spirit, which are God's.

— 1 Corinthians 6:19-20

More Verses
Romans 12:1; 1 Corinthians 6:13; 2 Corinthians 5:15

I have been chosen and appointed to bear fruit that remains

I did not chose Christ, but He has chosen **me**, and ordained **me**, that **I** should go and bring forth fruit, and that **my** fruit should remain. Whatever **I** will ask of the Father in Christ's name, He will give it to **me**.

— *John* 15:16

More Verses

Ephesians 2:10; Colossians 1:10;
2 Thessalonians 1:11

I am God's co-worker by His kindness

As God's co-worker, **I** should not toss aside this marvelous message of God's great kindness!

- 2 Corinthians 6:1

More Verses
1 Corinthians 3:9; Mark 16:20;
Philippians 2:13

Part Eight

I am...

Healed and Whole

My Identity In Christ

I am forgiven of all my iniquities, I am healed of all my diseases

Bless the LORD, O **my** soul, and forget not all His benefits: Who forgives all **my** iniquities; who heals all of **my** diseases.

- Psalm 103:2-3

More Verses
Psalm 147:3; Exodus 15:26;
Matthew 4:23; Psalm 91:16

I was healed by the stripes of Jesus. I am dead to sin and I live in righteousness

Christ bore **my** sins in His own body on the tree, that **I**, being dead to sins, should live unto righteousness: by whose stripes **I** was healed.

- 1 Peter 2:24

More Verses

Isaiah 53:5; Matthew 8:16-17; Psalm 107:20

Jesus took all my diseases and bore all my sicknesses

That it might be fulfilled which was spoken by Isaiah the prophet, saying, He took **my** infirmities and He bore **my** sicknesses.

— *Matthew* 8:17

More Verses
Isaiah 53:4; Acts 10:38;
Matthew 4:23

I am prosperous and in health, as my soul prospers

…**I** will prosper and be in health, even as **my** soul prospers.

- 3 John 1:2

More Verses
Psalm 35:27; Proverbs 4:20-22;
Deuteronomy 28:1-2

My health is restored to me and my wounds are healed

The Lord restores health to **me**, and heals **my** wounds…

- Jeremiah 30:17

More Verses
Deuteronomy 7:15; Romans 8:11; Psalm 107:20

My Identity In Christ

Part Nine

I am...

Equipped and Empowered

My Identity In Christ

I have God's power at work within me; He is able to do exceeding abundantly above all that I could ever ask or think

God is able to do exceeding abundantly above all that **I** ask or think, according to the power that works in **me**…

\- Ephesians 3:20

More Verses
Colossians 1:29; Philippians 2:13;
2 Corinthians 4:7

I have all grace abounding toward me, and am sufficient in all things

And God is able to make all grace abound toward **me**; that **I**, always having all sufficiency in all things, may abound to every good work.

- 2 Corinthians 9:8

More Verses
Philippians 4:19; 2 Corinthians 12:9;
Ephesians 2:10

I am strengthened with all might, according to God's glorious power

I am strengthened with all might, according to His glorious power, to all patience and long-suffering with joyfulness.

— Colossians 1:11

More Verses

Ephesians 6:10; Isaiah 40:31;
2 Timothy 2:1

I was made perfect and complete to do God's will, what I do is well-pleasing in His sight

[The Lord] has made **me** perfect in every good work to do His will, working in **me** that which is well-pleasing in His sight, through Jesus Christ…

- Hebrews 13:21

More Verses
Philippians 2:13; 2 Corinthians 3:5;
1 Thessalonians 5:23-24

I am God's workmanship, created in Christ Jesus for good works

For **I am** His workmanship, created
in Christ Jesus for good works,
which God ordained beforehand that
I should walk in them.

- Ephesians 2:10

More Verses
Titus 2:14; 2 Timothy 3:17;
James 2:17

I am blessed with every spiritual blessing in heavenly places in Christ

Blessed be the God and Father of our Lord Jesus Christ, who has blessed **me** with all spiritual blessings in heavenly places in Christ:

- Ephesians 1:3

More Verses
2 Peter 1:3; Philippians 4:19;
Colossians 2:10

I have direct access to God through the Holy Spirit

For through him **I** have access by one Spirit to the Father.

— Ephesians 2:18

More Verses

Hebrews 4:16; Romans 5:2;
Ephesians 3:12

I can approach God with freedom and confidence

In Christ and through faith in Him **I** may approach God with freedom and confidence.

- *Ephesians* 3:12

More Verses
Hebrews 10:19-22; Romans 5:2;
1 John 3:21

I have the mind of Christ

Who on earth knows the mind of the Lord? Who could ever know enough to teach Him? But **I** have the mind of Christ.

— 1 Corinthians 2:16

More Verses

Romans 12:2; Philippians 4:8; Colossians 3:2

I am God's temple

Don't **I** know that **I am** the temple of God, and that the Holy Spirit of God lives in **me**?

— 1 Corinthians 3:16

More Verses
1 Corinthians 6:19;
2 Corinthians 6:16; Ephesians 2:22

I am united with the Lord and have become one spirit with Him

I am united to the Lord and **I** have become one spirit with Him.

— 1 Corinthians 6:17

More Verses

John 15:4; 1 John 4:13; Romans 8:9

I am an ambassador for Christ

Therefore, **I am** an ambassador for Christ, God makes His appeals through **me**…

\- 2 Corinthians 5:20

More Verses
2 Corinthians 5:18-19;
Matthew 28:19-20; Romans 10:14-15

I am the salt and light of the earth

I am the salt of the earth… and **I am** the light of the world. A city that is set on an hill cannot be hid.

— Matthew 5:13-14

More Verses

Philippians 2:15; Ephesians 5:8;
1 Peter 2:12

I am a branch of the True Vine, a channel of His life

Jesus is the vine; **I am** the branches. When **I** abide in Christ and Christ in **me**, **I** bear much fruit, for apart from Christ **I** can do nothing.

- John 15:5

More Verses
John 15:4; Galatians 5:22-23;
Colossians 2:6

I can do all things through Christ who strengthens me

I can do all things through Christ who strengthens **me**.

- Philippians 4:13

More Verses

2 Corinthians 12:9; Isaiah 41:10;
Ephesians 6:10

As Christ is, so am I in this world

God's love is made perfect in **me**, **I** can be without fear on the day of judgement. **I** will be without fear, because in this world **I** am just like Jesus.

- 1 John 4:17

More Verses
Hebrews 4:16; Ephesians 3:12;
1 John 2:28

Part Ten

In Him

Scriptures

Verses to Study

My Identity In Christ

This book has only scratched the surface on your identity in Christ. The following section contains every verse in the New Testament that reveals your identity in Him. Verses in **bold** are the verses that were featured in this book. We encourage you to study these verses in your personal time with the Lord to learn more about who you are… in Him!

In Christ

Rom. 3:24	Gal. 2:4	Col. 1:28
Rom. 8:1	**Gal. 3:26**	1 Thes. 4:16
Rom. 8:2	Gal. 3:28	1 Thes. 5:18
Rom. 12:5	Gal. 5:6	1 Tim. 1:14
1 Cor. 1:2	Gal. 6:15	**2 Tim. 1:9**
1 Cor. 1:30	**Eph. 1:3**	**2 Tim. 1:12-13**
1 Cor. 15:22	Eph. 1:10	2 Tim. 2:1
1 Cor. 1:21	**Eph. 2:6**	2 Tim. 2:10
1 Cor. 2:14-16	**Eph. 2:10**	2 Tim. 3:15
1 Cor. 3:14	Eph. 2:13	**Phil. 1:6**
2 Cor. 5:17	Eph. 3:6	2 Peter 1:8
2 Cor. 5:19-20	Phil. 3:13-14	2 John 1:9

In Him

Acts 17:28	Col. 2:6	1 John 3:3
John 1:4	Col. 2:7	1 John 3:5
John 3:15-16	Col. 2:10	1 John 3:6
2 Cor. 1:20-22	1 John 2:5	1 John 3:24
2 Cor. 5:21	1 John 2:6	1 John 4:13
Eph. 1:4	1 John 2:8	**1 John 5:14-18**
Eph. 1:10	1 John 2:27	1 John 5:20
Phil. 3:9	1 John 2:28	

In the Beloved

Eph. 1:6

In the Lord

Eph. 5:8
Eph. 6:10

In Whom

Eph. 1:7	Eph. 2:22	Col. 2:11
Eph. 1:11	**Eph. 3:12**	1 Peter 1:8
Eph. 1:13	Col. 1:14	
Eph. 2:21	Col. 2:3	

By Christ

Rom. 3:22	2 Cor. 5:18	1 Peter 1:3
Rom. 5:15	Gal. 2:16	1 Peter 2:5
Rom. 5:17-19	Eph. 1:5	1 Peter 5:10
Rom. 7:4	Phil. 1:11	
1 Cor. 1:4	Phil. 4:19	

By Him

1 Cor. 1:5	Col. 1:17	**Heb. 7:25**
1 Cor. 8:6	Col. 1:20	Heb. 13:15
Col. 1:16	Col. 3:17	1 Peter 1:21

By Himself

Heb. 1:3   Heb. 9:26

By His Blood

Heb. 9:11-12   Heb. 10:19-20
Heb. 9:14-15   1 John 1:7

By Whom

Rom. 5:2   Rom 5:11   Gal. 6:14

From Whom

Eph. 4:16   Col. 2:19

Of Christ

2 Cor. 2:15   Col. 2:17
Phil. 3:12   Col. 3:24

Of Him

1 John 1:5   1 John 2:27

Through Christ

Rom. 5:1	**1 Cor. 15:57**	Phil. 4:6-7
Rom. 5:11	Gal. 3:13-14	**Phil. 4:13**
Rom. 6:11	**Gal. 4:7**	**Heb. 10:10**
Rom. 6:23	Eph. 2:7	**Heb. 13:20-21**

Through Him

John 3:17	**Rom. 8:37**	1 John 4:9
Rom. 5:9	**Eph. 2:18**	

With Christ

Rom. 6:8	Eph. 2:5	Col. 3:1
Gal. 2:20	Col. 2:20	Col. 3:3

With Him

Rom. 6:8	Eph. 2:5	Col. 3:1
Gal. 2:20	Col. 2:20	Col. 3:3

By Me

John 6:57   John 14:6

In Me

John 6:56   **John 15:4-5**   **John 16:33**
John 14:20   John 15:7-8

In My Love

John 15:9

In His Name

Mat. 18:20   John 14:13-14   **1 Cor. 6:11-20**
Mark 16:17-18   John 16:23-24

Other Scriptures

The following verses may not use the phrases listed above, but they convey the message of who you are because of Christ.

Mat. 8:17	**Rom. 8:14-17**	Heb. 10:14
Mat. 11:28-30	Gal. 3:29	Heb. 13:5-6
Mat. 18:11	Gal. 5:1	Heb. 13:8
Mat. 18:18-20	**Eph. 4:24**	James 4:7
Mat. 28:18-20	Phil. 2:5	**1 Peter 2:9**
Mark 1:8	Phil. 2:13	1 Peter 2:21
Mark 9:23	Col. 1:13	1 Peter 3:18
Mark 11:23-24	Col. 1:26-27	1 Peter 5:7
Luke 10:19	Titus 2:14	**2 Peter 1:4**
John 4:14	Titus 3:7	1 John 1:9
John 5:24	Heb. 2:9-11	1 John 2:1
John 6:40	Heb. 2:14-15	1 John 3:2
John 10:10	Heb. 2:18	1 John 3:14
John 14:12	Heb. 4:14-16	**1 John 4:4**
John 14:23	Heb. 7:19,22	**1 John 4:9-10**
John 15:15	Heb. 8:6	**1 John 4:15**
John 17:23	**Heb. 8:12**	**1 John 5:1,4-5**
Rom. 5:5	Heb. 9:24	1 John 5:11-12
Rom. 6:4	Heb. 9:28	Rev. 1:5-6

Confession of My Identity in Christ

Heavenly Father, in the name of Jesus, I come boldly before Your throne of grace, knowing that I am accepted in the Beloved and made righteous through Christ (Ephesians 1:6; 2 Corinthians 5:21). I thank You that I am a new creation in Christ Jesus; old things have passed away and all things have become new (2 Corinthians 5:17). I declare by faith that I am born of God, filled with Your Spirit, and called according to Your purpose (Romans 8:28).

Father, Your Word says that I am chosen, holy, and dearly loved (Colossians 3:12). You chose me in Christ before the foundation of the world, that I should be holy and blameless before You in love (Ephesians 1:4). I thank You that I am not rejected, forgotten, or overlooked—I am adopted as Your child, and by Your Spirit I cry, "Abba, Father" (Romans 8:15). Your Spirit bears witness with my spirit that I am a child of God and an heir of Your promises (Romans 8:16–17).

Lord, I declare that I am seated with Christ in heavenly places (Ephesians 2:6). I have been delivered from the power of darkness and translated into the kingdom of Your dear Son (Colossians 1:13). Sin no longer has dominion over me, for I am under grace (Romans 6:14). I walk in the liberty where Christ has made me free (Galatians 5:1), and whom the Son sets free is free indeed (John 8:36).

Father, I thank You that I am the righteousness of God in Christ Jesus (2 Corinthians 5:21). I have peace with You through my Lord Jesus Christ (Romans 5:1). I do not live under condemnation, because there is now no condemnation for those who are in Christ Jesus (Romans 8:1). Your grace empowers me to live in victory, and Your Spirit leads me in the paths of life.

I declare that I am strong in the Lord and in the power of His might (Ephesians 6:10). Greater is He who is in me than he who is in the world (1 John 4:4). I overcome by the blood of the Lamb and by the word of my testimony (Revelation 12:11). Through Christ I am more than a conqueror (Romans 8:37), and I can do all things through Christ who strengthens me (Philippians 4:13).

Father, Your Word is alive in me. I renew my mind to Your truth, and Your truth makes me free (John 8:32; Romans 12:2). Your Word is a lamp to my feet and a light to my path (Psalm 119:105). I declare that the same Spirit who raised Jesus from the dead lives in me and gives life to my body and strength to my spirit (Romans 8:11).

Thank You, Father, that I am blessed with every spiritual blessing in the heavenly places in Christ (Ephesians 1:3). I walk in the calling You have placed on my life. I am Your workmanship, created in Christ Jesus for good works which You prepared beforehand for me to walk in (Ephesians 2:10). I will fulfill the purpose You have for me, and Your grace is sufficient in every area of my life.

I receive these truths by faith, and I boldly declare that my identity is found in Christ alone. I am redeemed, forgiven, empowered, and loved. I give You all the praise and glory, Father, in the mighty name of Jesus—Amen.

PRAYER FOR SALVATION AND BAPTISM IN THE HOLY SPIRIT

Heavenly Father, I come to You now in the Name of Jesus. Your Word says that, if I will call on the name of the Lord, I will be saved (Acts 2:21). I am calling on You. I pray and confess Jesus as Lord over my life according to Romans 10:9-10: "If you will confess with your mouth the Lord Jesus, and believe in your heart that God has raised him from the dead, you will be saved. For with the heart man believes to righteousness; and with the mouth confession is made to salvation." I do that now. I confess that Jesus is Lord, and I believe in my heart that God raised Him from the dead.

I am now reborn! I am a Christian—a child of Almighty God! I am saved!

You also said in your Word, "...HOW MUCH MORE will your heavenly Father give the Holy Spirit to them that ask him?" (Luke 11:13). I'm asking now... fill me with your Holy Spirit. Holy Spirit, rise up within me as I praise God. I fully expect to speak with other tongues as you give me the utterance (Acts 2:4). In Jesus Name, Amen!

Begin to praise God for filling you with the Holy Spirit. Speak those words and syllables you receive—not in your own language, but the language given to you by the Holy Spirit. You have to use your own voice. God will not force you to speak. Don't be concerned with how it sounds. It is a heavenly language!

Praise God! You are a healed, born-again, Spirit-filled believer. You'll never be the same again. Find a good church that boldly preaches God's Word and obeys it. Become part of a church family who will love and care for you as you love and care for them.

MyVersion Publishing

We hope you enjoyed this personalized declarations book. Looking for more customized scripture topics like healing, peace, or finances? Maybe you'd like to own the personalized book you just read in audiobook or ebook format?

MyVersion Publishing offers ebooks, audiobooks, and paperback books just like this one in 100's of popular male and female names as well as in personalized "I am" confessions.

You can find your name or your friend's name on Amazon or custom order a name on our website at MyVersionBook.com, these mini-books are a convenient 4x6 inch pocket-sized paperback, ebook, audiobook, or Kindle ebook; perfect for gift-giving or keeping in your pocket as a source of encouragement wherever you go.

Visit our website now to get your custom, personalized books!